THIS OR THAT? History Edition

Surviving the SANTA FE TRAIL
A This or That Debate

by Jessica Rusick

CAPSTONE PRESS
a capstone imprint

Capstone Captivate is published by Capstone Press, an imprint of Capstone.
1710 Roe Crest Drive
North Mankato, Minnesota 56003
www.capstonepub.com

Library of Congress Cataloging-in-Publication Data is available on the Library of Congress website.
ISBN: 978-1-4966-8391-5 (library binding)
ISBN: 978-1-4966-8789-0 (paperback)
ISBN: 978-1-4966-8442-4 (eBook PDF)

Summary: The Santa Fe Trail was a route used by traders, pioneers, and the military in the 1800s. Test your decision-making skills by answering this or that questions about traveling the trail!

Image Credits
Flickr: British Library, 15, David Herrera, 10, Forest Service, 20, Internet Archive Book Images, 7, 18, © Samat Jain, used CC BY-SA 2.0., 11; Gift of Mrs. E. V. Anderson, 1943/The Metropolitan Museum of Art, 26; iStockphoto: Alysta, 24, bauhaus1000, 9, CarbonBrain, 25, duncan1890, 29, ilbusca, 13, KenWiedemann, 28, ktmoffitt, 17, StudioBarcelona, 6; Library of Congress: Ritchie & Dunnavant, 32, Cover (map); Shutterstock: Africa Studio, 22, Andy Wilcock, 23, Artic_photo, 21, Brave_Creative, 12, Canicula, 16, Eric Isselee, 30, Felipe Sanchez, Cover (blanket), Jill Lang, Cover (wagon), Mike Flippo, Cover (sombrero), Quinn Calder, Cover (longhorn), Solphoto, Cover (Tent Rocks National Monument), Zoran Milic, 5 (map); Wikimedia Commons: Ammodramus, 19, California Historical Society Collection, 1860-1960, Title Insurance and Trust, and C.C. Pierce Photography Collection, 1860-1960, Miss Annette Glick Collection/U.S. National Archives and Records Administration, 8, Commissioned by William T. Walters, 1858-1860/Walters Art Museum, 14, Daderot, 27, Internet Archive Book Images, 4–5, Larry Lamsa, 3

Design Elements: Library of Congress: Ritchie & Dunnavant (background map)

Editorial Credits
Editor: Rebecca Felix; Designers: Aruna Rangarajan & Tamara JM Peterson; Production Specialist: Tori Abraham

A TRAIL FOR TRADERS

The Santa Fe Trail was established in 1821. It connected Missouri to Santa Fe, New Mexico. Traders traveled the trail carrying goods to trade.

Traders carried goods on animals and in wagons. The journey took eight weeks and covered about 900 miles (1,450 kilometers). Travelers faced accidents, buffalo **stampedes**, and storms along the way.

As the trail grew popular, **pioneers** and the U.S. military also used it. However, by 1880, western railroads provided easier travel. The Santa Fe Trail was no longer used.

HOW TO USE THIS BOOK

What if you had been a traveler on the Santa Fe Trail? What choices would you have made along the way? Do you think you would have survived?

This book is full of questions that relate to the Santa Fe Trail. Some are questions real people had to face. The questions are followed by details to help you come to a decision.

THE SANTA FE TRAIL

Missouri

New Mexico

KEY

Trail ◄--

N
W ◆ E
S

Pick one choice or the other. There are no wrong answers! But just like the travelers, you should think carefully about your decisions.

Are you ready? Turn the page to pick this or that!

To carry your goods using PACK ANIMALS?

➤ can't carry as much as a wagon

➤ must stop often

➤ risk of animals getting injured

Some early traders on the trail used **pack animals** to carry goods. Traders had to stop often so the animals could rest after carrying so much weight. Even so, the animals could travel faster than wagons. However, the animals couldn't hold as much as wagons, so traders couldn't make as much money in trades.

To carry your goods using
WAGON CARAVANS?

➤ can carry more

➤ harder to move around obstacles

➤ wagons could be taxed

Wagons could hold thousands of pounds of goods. This meant traders could make more money in Santa Fe. But some years, traders had to pay a tax on each wagon before trading. It was also harder to **maneuver** wagons over rocks and across rivers. A whole team might have to help lift a wagon out of mud or steady it over a large rock.

To have
MULES PULL YOUR WAGON?

- ➤ faster than oxen, but worse tempers
- ➤ have to carry extra food for them
- ➤ less likely to starve in the desert

Traders used oxen or mules to pull wagons. Mules were faster than oxen, but not as strong. They were also more likely to kick people or refuse to move. Mules needed to eat grain as well as prairie grass. This meant traders had to carry the grain as well as trade goods. But grain meant mules were less likely to **starve** in the desert.

To have
OXEN PULL YOUR WAGON?

> slower than mules, but better tempers

> don't have to carry extra food for them

> more likely to starve in the desert

Oxen were slow, but strong. Oxen also had better tempers than mules. And unlike mules, oxen could also survive on prairie grass. This meant traders didn't have to carry extra food. However, it also meant oxen could starve if stretches of the trail were without grass.

Would you choose . . .

THIS

To take the
MOUNTAIN ROUTE?

➤ longer than Cimarron Route

➤ must pass through mountains

➤ more water sources

The trail split into two main paths. The Mountain Route required a trip through tall, dangerous peaks. Travelers had to guide their wagons and animals over large boulders. They might travel only 3,000 feet (914 meters) a day. However, the Mountain Route had more water sources, saving travelers from thirst.

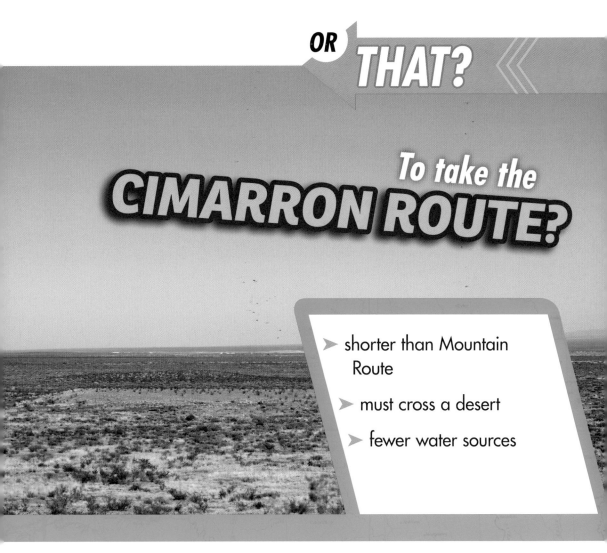

To take the
CIMARRON ROUTE?

- ➤ shorter than Mountain Route
- ➤ must cross a desert
- ➤ fewer water sources

The Cimarron Route was 100 miles (161 km) shorter than the Mountain Route. However, it crossed a desert with little water to drink or grass to feed animals. Travelers had to have detailed knowledge of where the few water sources were. Otherwise, these sources were almost impossible to find. People and animals could easily die of thirst along this route.

Would you choose . . .

THIS

To run BENT'S FORT?

- ➤ overrun with soldiers
- ➤ travelers ruin the land
- ➤ might have to abandon fort

Bent's Fort was a fur trading post along the trail where traders and Native Americans traded goods. But in 1846, the United States went to war with Mexico. During the Mexican-American War, American soldiers marched along the trail and stayed at Bent's Fort without paying. They also **polluted** nearby land and overused the fort's resources.

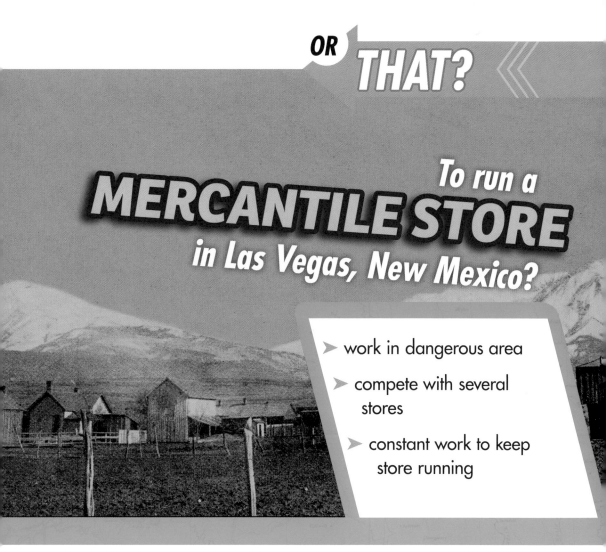

To run a **MERCANTILE STORE** in Las Vegas, New Mexico?

➤ work in dangerous area

➤ compete with several stores

➤ constant work to keep store running

Mercantile stores sold supplies and food to travelers along the trail. One store was in Las Vegas, New Mexico. This was a dangerous place. Gunfights happened in the streets. Las Vegas also had several mercantile stores. This meant a shop owner had to **convince** customers to shop at his or her store instead of the others. If owners didn't do this, their stores could go out of business.

Would you choose . . .

THIS

To use the trail as a
FUR TRAPPER?

- ➤ carry your own supplies
- ➤ work alone
- ➤ hunt for your own food

Fur trappers trapped animals and traded their furs. Trappers worked alone. This meant there was no one to help if they were injured in an accident. Trappers also caught and cooked animals to eat. Their meals depended on how well they could hunt. If game was scarce, trappers ate wild plants or even boiled leather to survive.

To use the trail as a
MEXICAN-AMERICAN WAR SOLDIER?

➤ lack of supplies
➤ fights
➤ limited food

In the Mexican-American War, American soldiers fought in battles against Mexican soldiers. American soldiers had supply wagons on the trail. But supplies were not always given correctly. Some soldiers didn't get tents or eating **utensils**. Fights broke out when soldiers stole supplies from each other. Soldiers were also ordered to **ration** food so it would last. Sometimes dinner was only a bit of bread.

Would you choose . . .

THIS

To serve as a SCOUT?

- ➤ ride ahead of wagon train
- ➤ alone or with one other person
- ➤ little protection

Scouts rode ahead of their party to look for water sources and check if rivers were too high to cross. They rode back to the group to share the information. Scouts rode alone or in pairs. With little protection, they were at risk of attacks from **thieves**. If scouts were injured, they had to wait for the group to catch up before receiving help or care.

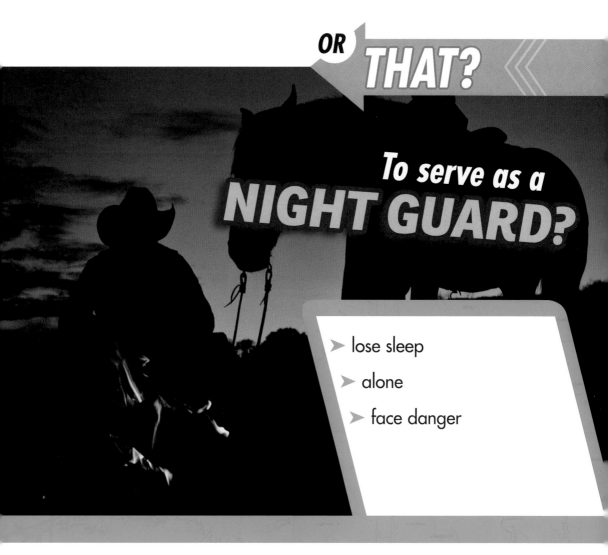

OR THAT?

To serve as a
NIGHT GUARD?

➤ lose sleep

➤ alone

➤ face danger

Night guards watched over their group at night. The guards were the first defense against any danger. Travelers guarded in shifts. Depending on the shift, a guard could be up much of the night. This would make traveling the next day even more exhausting. Lack of sleep also led to mistakes. One night guard accidentally shot his mule because he thought it was a thief.

Would you choose . . .

THIS

To travel with William Becknell on his FIRST TRIP to Santa Fe?

➤ small group

➤ danger from thieves

➤ rocks along route

William Becknell first traveled the Santa Fe Trail in 1821 with four or five other men. This small number did not provide much protection from thieves. The group rode horses, whose feet were sensitive to rocks. The trail wasn't a cleared road. At one point, Becknell spent two days clearing rocks for the horses.

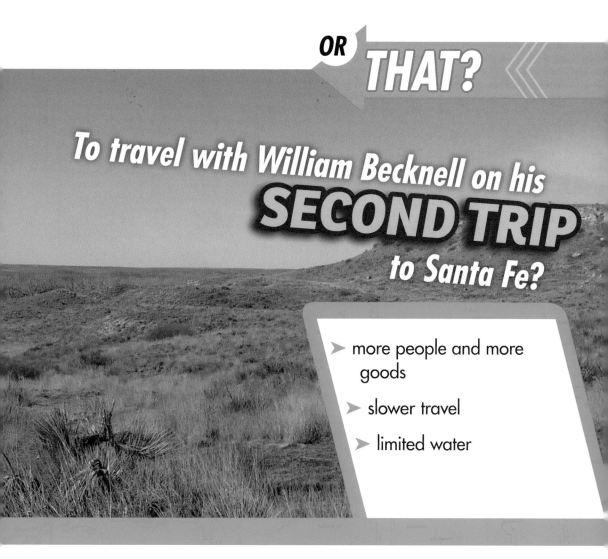

To travel with William Becknell on his **SECOND TRIP** to Santa Fe?

> more people and more goods
> slower travel
> limited water

Becknell traveled with 21 men and three wagons on his second trail trip in 1822. The wagons and extra help meant he could carry more goods. But this also slowed his travel. Becknell took a different route on this trip in hopes of traveling faster. But he didn't have a map of water sources. As a result, his group nearly died from thirst in the desert. To survive, they killed a buffalo and drank the water in its stomach!

THIS

To FORD a swollen river?

- ➤ must avoid quicksand
- ➤ scares animals
- ➤ safer to move quickly, but this depended on animals

Fording meant walking wagons and animals across the river. Scouts went ahead to check for **quicksand**. Fording wasn't usually dangerous if done quickly. But animals could get scared in water. Then travelers would have to ford each one individually. This took extra time and increased the chances of accidental drowning.

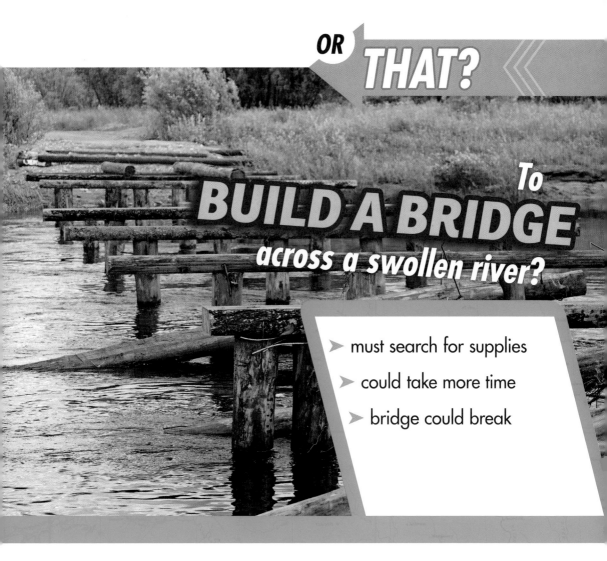

To **BUILD A BRIDGE** across a swollen river?

➤ must search for supplies

➤ could take more time

➤ bridge could break

Some travelers built bridges instead of fording. This took time. The group sent people ahead to make the bridge from wood and prairie grasses. Bridges usually kept trade goods, animals, and people safe. But if the bridge wasn't sturdy enough, it could break. This would send the entire party crashing into the water.

Would you choose . . .

THIS

To travel with the
BAIRD-CHAMBERS PARTY?

- ➤ stuck in cold
- ➤ animals die
- ➤ must leave goods behind

The Baird-Chambers party traveled the trail in 1822. Its members got caught in a snowstorm. They were stranded in the cold for three months! Most of their animals died, leaving the group members without a way to transport their goods. They buried the goods and trekked to Taos, New Mexico, to buy more animals. They returned to dig up their goods before continuing to Santa Fe.

To travel with
BENJAMIN COOPER'S PARTY?

➤ animals stolen

➤ no water in desert

➤ become tired looking for water

Benjamin Cooper's party traveled the trail in 1823. Early one morning, thieves stole many of the group's horses and mules. The thieves fired guns to frighten the animals and drive them away from the camp. Later, the Cooper party ran out of water in the desert. The group got so thirsty it cut its mules' ears to drink the animals' blood.

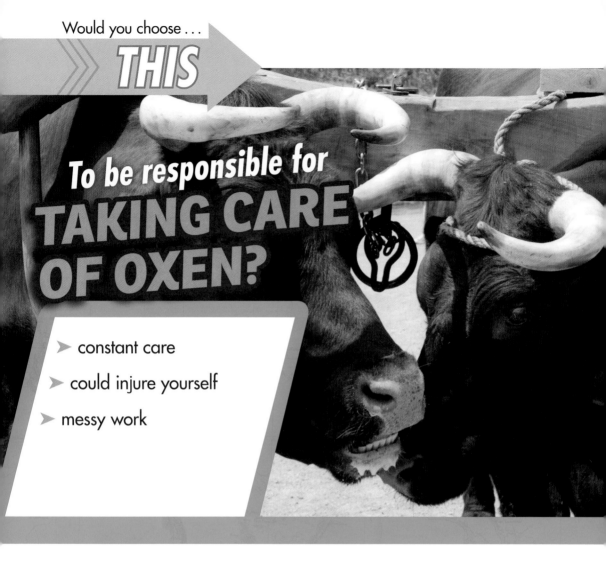

THIS

To be responsible for
TAKING CARE OF OXEN?

➤ constant care

➤ could injure yourself

➤ messy work

Caring for animals on the trail was hard work. Oxen had to be **shod**. This involved using hot tar to stick buffalo hide to the animals' hooves. The task put you at risk of burning your hands. Dust could also make it hard for oxen to breathe. You'd have to wipe their eyes, noses, and tongues with rags. This could make you dirty and slobbery.

To be responsible for
COOKING THE DAY'S MAIN MEAL?

➤ messy

➤ handle fresh animal meat

➤ touch buffalo poop

Trail cooking was messy work. It often involved **butchering** animals. You'd also have to build a fire to cook over. In some places, there wasn't wood to make fire. Instead, travelers gathered dried patties of buffalo poop with their bare hands. The poop burned well. Luckily, it didn't smell as it burned.

THIS

To wear SHOES?

➤ heavy

➤ hard to walk in

➤ can hurt feet

Typical shoes in the 1800s were leather with thick, heavy soles that made them inflexible. It was uncomfortable to walk long distances in them. The shoes also rubbed against traders' feet, causing blisters and calluses. These were made worse when the shoes got wet. Travelers had to wear thick socks to protect themselves from the shoes.

To wear
MOCCASINS?

> lightweight
> might have to make your own replacements
> could shrink

Moccasins are shoes made from soft animal hide. Traders found them light and easy to walk in. They could also be lined with soft or warm material like fur. But moccasins wore out quickly along the trail. Some traders made replacement moccasins as they traveled. If this wasn't done properly, the moccasins could shrink around their feet as they walked.

Would you choose . . .

THIS

To help

PULL A WAGON OUT OF MUD *during a rainstorm?*

➤ get dirty from mud

➤ hard work

➤ could get injured

In a bad rainstorm, wagon wheels could sink into mud and become stuck. To raise a wagon, many people had to put their hands on its wheels and lift. This was dangerous. You could slip in the mud or sink into it yourself. If you weren't careful, you could also get crushed by the heavy wagon.

OR THAT?

To LOOK FOR LOST ANIMALS during a rainstorm?

➤ lost, scared animals can be unpredictable

➤ face dangers while looking for them

➤ slows down trip if you can't find them

Animals could get scared during rainstorms and run away. It could be dangerous to look for them, especially at night. You too could get lost. You could also run into wild animals. If you couldn't find the lost animals, you wouldn't have as many to transport your goods.

LIGHTNING ROUND

Would you choose to . . .

➤ eat spoiled meat or drink spoiled milk?

➤ camp in the open air to see the night sky or in a tent to stay a bit warmer?

➤ have your clothes ruined or some of your trade goods ruined?

➤ run out of salt or sugar for meals?

➤ get your leg kicked by a mule or your foot run over by a wagon wheel?

➤ eat buffalo bone marrow or beaver tail?

➤ face a buffalo stampede or a rattlesnake?

➤ have an extra change of clothes or an extra set of eating utensils?

GLOSSARY

butcher (BUCH-ur)—to cut up meat

convince (kuhn-VINS)—to persuade someone to do or believe something

maneuver (muh-NOO-vur)—to move something carefully

pack animal (PAK AN-uh-mul)—an animal that can carry heavy supplies

pioneer (pye-uh-NEER)—a person who explores unknown territory and settles there

polluted (puh-LOOT-ed)—contaminated or made dirty or impure, especially with waste

quicksand (KWIK-sand)—loose, wet sand that is dangerous because a person or items can sink into it

ration (RASH-uhn)—to give something out in limited amounts

shod (SHAHD)—to provide or fit with shoes

stampede (stam-PEED)—a sudden, wild rush in one direction, usually out of fear

starve (STAHRV)—suffering or dying from lack of food

thief (THEEF)—a person who steals others' belongings or money

utensil (yoo-TEN-suhl)—a tool often used in the kitchen and for a special purpose

READ MORE

Harris, Irene. *The Homestead Act and Westward Expansion: Settling the Western Frontier*. New York: PowerKids Press, 2017.

Stoltman, Joan. *20 Fun Facts About Westward Expansion*. New York: Gareth Stevens Publishing, 2019.

Williams, Jean K. *The Perils of the Santa Fe Trail*. North Mankato, MN: Capstone Press, a Capstone imprint, 2018.

INTERNET SITES

Ducksters—Westward Expansion: Mexican-American War
https://www.ducksters.com/history/westward_expansion/mexican-american_war.php

Kiddle—Santa Fe Trail Facts for Kids
https://kids.kiddle.co/Santa_Fe_Trail

Santa Fe Trail Association—Junior Wagon Master
https://www.santafetrail.org/children/jr-wagon-master.html